This book is dedicated to those who have tried to quit smoking and failed. It is dedicated to those who know how hard it can be and deep down never believed it was possible for them. It is dedicated to the hardest smokers with the worst possible habits and very possibly to you or someone you love.

HOW TO QUIT SMOKING
LIKE A COWARD

End the habit in a way that's painless, enjoyable and for good.

CHAPTER 1

Sometimes in life, you experience something so life changing and profound, it seems a crime to keep it to yourself.

A few years ago, you could say, that I invented a method for quitting smoking that was completely painless, eliminated the withdrawal symptoms and left the results permanent. I can attest to that permanence, as the final edit for this book was made around eight years later.

To understand why quitting smoking was so huge for me, you first have to understand how ingrained the smoking habit was embedded in my life. This should also give you an idea of how you might compare if you choose to undertake this journey.

I smoked a pack of cigarettes a day for almost sixteen years. On nights out, or at parties with friends, I would sometimes smoke almost two boxes of twenty cigarettes. I loved to smoke and lived in a reality where deep down I never believed I would ever stop. The times I toyed with that possibility, were when I was forced not to smoke for a longer than normal period due to a work-related matter, but that was followed by a happy relapse back into the satisfaction and relaxation that smoking provided for me.

In fact, those gaps without cigarettes just made them more satisfying for me.

It got worse. And I'm really going to paint myself in a bad light here, so you'll have to bear with me here. Aside from my regular box of cigarettes, I had a pipe for a while. I'd smoke unfiltered tobacco in it, marijuana too. I rolled my own cigarettes at one point, and here comes one of my lowest points of my life. I remember at one time, I was so poor, I couldn't afford cigarettes or anything else for that matter, and I remember picking up cigarette butts off the street to roll them into rolling papers I had, just so I could smoke. Now, I'm not proud of that, nor am I particularly keen on making that public knowledge, but if I truly want to help anyone, you'll will need to know how bad the habit was and how desperately I needed to smoke to maintain my sanity.

When I did eventually sort out my finances, I bought and hoarded cigarettes. My pride was not going to let me be in that position again.

At a more stable point in life, I remember seeing people I know, kicking the habit and I liked how happy they were when they spoke about it. Motivated by being tired of the feeling in my lungs and how dirty the habit is, having ashtrays around and everything reeking of smoke, I investigated some of the planet's most popular programs about quitting smoking. Being the person I am, I've always known I could always accomplish anything with the right education and time to master the principles. However, after reading a popular book on the topic, which prescribed a ceremonial last cigarette and then never looking back, I discovered a harsh truth which I learned the hard way.

This realisation was that withdrawal symptoms are very real and very painful. While some people can just shake it off and suffer through all the way, my habit was so much a part of my life, I simply could not do it. The pain and discomfort I experienced during that time was far beyond anything I could have imagined.

Seven days into an absolute cold turkey leaving behind my lifelong companion, I developed the worst withdrawal symptoms I have ever experienced in my life. At the time, I experienced a total disconnection from my body, and nothing seemed to satisfy me at all. And I mean nothing. Food, sex, anything that brought me a sense of wellbeing, happiness or release was completely empty. If my head itched, even scratching it would provide no relief. It's safe to say that this is among the top ten worst experiences of my life. The psychology and mental resolve were there, the unbending intent to kick the habit, however, dealing with the chemistry, was another matter entirely.

It was at this point a friend phoned me, and on hearing my account of the horror and misery I was experiencing, he advised that I smoke a cigarette. They suggested that cold turkey is maybe not the most effective way to quit and that it would be better to slowly cut down before you intend to quit. At that point, I would have taken any course of action to feel better, so I walked into the nearest convenience store, bought a single cigarette, and smoked it.

Immediately, my symptoms disappeared, so I bought another three and smoked two of them on the spot.

While my ego was bruised at having failed my quest, knowing now I would probably go deeper into the habit, another part of me didn't care as I didn't have to feel those terrible feelings anymore.

I also secretly resented my friend, blaming him for being the one who put the idea in my head, giving me the 'out'. Years later, I realise he was right and advised me correctly.

I heard stories of people that become sick from quitting smoking as their body battled to adapt to the changes in their chemistry, and then I really understood why. If you also believe that your emotional well-being is a guide as to whether you are heading in the right direction, you can see that this was simply not the right answer for me.

After the events I've just described, I lapsed into another spree of smoking for several years, perhaps even more assured now that I'd never quit, having had first-hand experience of what could happen. I can easily admit that I was absolutely terrified of feeling that way again and knew there was no way I would ever subject myself to feeling that way again. The fear was so intense that I can't even remember what got me to consider trying again.

Thinking back, I remember that this was not my first attempt in quitting. I remember trying nicotine patches which didn't seem to work for me at all. I remembered trying the nicotine chewing gum as well. A few times. My experience was always that the gum with nicotine tasted really bad and the taste used to stick in my throat, so I never managed to get past chewing more than two or three pieces before I abandoned the idea altogether.

Throughout the years, I met some incredible people who just kicked the habit, usually cold turkey and marvelled at their resolve and ability to endure such suffering. I can only conclude that they were either just stronger than me, I was too sensitive, or assuming neither, perhaps I simply just smoked more than them.

Whatever the case, I knew had no hope of ever quitting, until casually one day, I had an idea. I felt that this idea was working through me and was somehow not even mine. It felt like a spark of inspiration that moved me to act. Not knowing where it would lead, I almost watched the process unfold, enjoying every step of the way.

CHAPTER 2

Even though I never had words for it at the time, if I had to put this idea in words, it would have been, 'What if I could quit smoking gradually over six months by steadily reducing my nicotine intake?'

I started to do some research into the chemicals that are absorbed into the body when smoking cigarettes and discovered that around 367 different harmful chemicals are absorbed into the bloodstream every time you smoke. The information I found was generally associated with manufacturers of electronic cigarettes who claimed that using their product would reduce the amount of chemicals taken into the body by at least a good 350. Another article mentioned that there are around 7000 chemicals in tobacco smoke, 250 of which are harmful and 69 of those which cause cancer.

While these numbers and facts were quite interesting to me, I knew deep down that the key enemy here was nicotine and this was a drug addiction I was dealing with.

I also remember at the time speaking someone who mentioned an oral fixation, a term I had never heard of before, so I did a bit of research and discovered that there is a sensory addiction as well that smokers must overcome in addition to the chemical addiction, although I believed that this was secondary.

So, having no idea of how I was going to overcome these odds, I set a few things in motion and made my mind up that I was going to do this, but without suffering one bit. It was more of an experiment than a plan. I bought an electronic cigarette from a reputable manufacturer and also asked people that used them what their experience was like making the transition. I received a very similar response from the people I asked, which was that after a day or two, they barely noticed a difference and were quite comfortable with the electronic cigarette, experiencing no unusual withdrawal symptoms as the electronic cigarettes still delivered the body with the nicotine that it needed.

I was however not ready to take that step yet. So, I left my electronic cigarette in my bedroom cupboard waiting for the day I would make the transition.

The next thing I did, was to instead of buying one packet of cigarettes, to buy two. Yes, you read that correctly. I used to smoke a heavy brand of cigarette that was rated at 1.8mg of nicotine per cigarette. I'd buy one box of those and then also a second box with half the nicotine rating. So, for instance, the red version of the brand for the stronger cigarette and then the blue version which was much lighter. At home, I'd divide each box in half, placing ten cigarettes of each into each box. So, I would have ten strong ones and ten lighter ones in each box.

In my day-to-day activities, I would continue to smoke as usual. If I felt like a good cigarette, I'd smoke a strong one. Otherwise, if I just needed a break or whenever I felt up to it, I'd smoke one of the lighter brand. In the beginning, there were times that after smoking the lighter brand, I didn't experience enough satisfaction, so I'd smoke two instead and I allowed that to be ok and not to beat myself up about it. In fact, I was having more fun smoking, because I had accessorised my smoking into a game that I had no idea if I could win or not.

After a month or two, I discovered a strange thing start to happen. My usual brand seemed to be a little heavy for what my body needed. I felt I was reaching a point where I could switch to the lighter brand and waited until I was absolutely sure. When the time came, I bought only the lighter brand and smoked only that for a few weeks.

Sometimes, I had to smoke two cigarettes in a row. If I was exceptionally irritable, I pulled the filter out with my teeth, which is surprising easy to do, split that in half lengthwise, folded it in half and re-inserted it into the cigarette, essentially in my mind making it twice as strong.

If that is a bit confusing, you could simply just cut off a bit of the filter with a scissors making it stronger.

It wasn't long before the half strength cigarette become my new normal and I hadn't suffered one bit, because I did it slowly and at my own pace. I was also strangely invigorated, as I knew that if I smoked the same amount of cigarettes a day, which was around fifteen to twenty, I was taking in half the nicotine I usually did.

The personal victory here was really good for my ego, but I'd like to share something I feel is almost vital to the success of the story. And that is I didn't tell anyone. Partly, because I knew that if I failed, which I had so many times, no-one could say a thing or give me any judging looks, but also because I was experimenting. In hindsight, I remember observing countless times how I, and others proclaimed loudly and publicly that they were going to do something and then proceeded not to succeed at doing that.

Often, it was the person that was saying I'm quitting smoking that failed, while the person that told no-one, had the resolve to do it, without needing any approval or validation from anyone else. I'd also add here that if anyone did ask, I had a plan to say I'm trying out a new brand. Which I recall maybe happened a few times while I was fumbling around for the right cigarette. The key was, I never told anyone I was quitting smoking and I suggest that would be the most effective strategy here.

I'd like to also at this point of my story add something I found tremendously beneficial. I believe that at some point in the journey of someone who wishes to quit smoking, it will be time to start making friends with good old-fashioned air again. To any smoker, I can imagine, that this thought is not as appealing as it sounds. However, here is how I did it, once again painless and without any suffering.

I had access to some basis exercise equipment on the roof of the building where I stayed. There were some walking machines plus a bike for spinning which I started to use. Having not necessarily been an exercise freak at all, I treated this very light heartedly. I would cycle to get my heart rate and breathing up, enjoy breaking a sweat and then head back home to enjoy an amazing cigarette after the workout. In fact, exercising made my cigarettes taste even better than before and I loved the head rush after a gym session. The idea here was not to overdo it and overexert myself in the gym, so I could go back the next day and the day after. I wanted to do things slowly and I was enjoying the process. Why I mention this, is that I believe the extra air and light cardio really helped in the process of cutting down the need for nicotine.

Meanwhile, having enjoyed such success and fuelled with inspiration at having halved my nicotine intake, I tried to repeat the formula again. I bought the half nicotine valued brand of cigarette at 0.9mg and then another box with a value of 0.4mg. This time, it was not so easy, and I felt I jumped the gun a little, so I kept the lighter cigarettes in the cupboard until I was ready to try again. A few weeks later and perhaps after a little more cardio, I added the lighter cigarettes into my daily routine, repeating the same process I used with the previous heavier brand. After a few weeks I found that a similar thing happened and I started to find the half strength cigarettes a little strong, naturally moving to the lighter brand.

After making this new much lighter brand my default cigarette and reaching a comfortable plateau again, I repeated the process yet again, including a second brand of 0,1mg to my daily routine and again alternating between the 0,4mg and 0,1mg brand. In hindsight, I would probably just omit this step to anyone that wants to follow a similar process and just move onto the step in the next chapter. For me, the 0,1mg cigarettes were very difficult to obtain any satisfaction from and even though I managed to do it, I felt it was unnecessary.

In my experiences in the gym, I always looked forward to my after-gym cigarette, but there were times where I would find smoking quite repulsive. At times, I'd smoke only half the cigarette and put it out, smoking it later on.

I had made some amazing progress so far and it was time to move onto

ANDREW AVVAKOUMIDES

the next step.

CHAPTER 3

By now, I had cut down my nicotine intake significantly and I hadn't told anyone what I was doing. I felt that the method I was working on was building a silent confidence in myself and my ability to actually get it done, so I didn't need to tell anybody anything. I felt that if I did eventually win, and I was never completely sure I would, I would wait a month before I told anybody. Or never tell anybody at all and be extraordinarily cool.

So, it was at this point, that I decided to switch to the electronic cigarette and move away the conventional cigarettes altogether.

This was surprisingly easy.

Seeing that most electronic cigarettes have a fairly high nicotine value in their highest doses, it almost felt like a relapse. The body was getting more nicotine than it was accustomed to, but now was 350 other chemicals less. After a day of using the electronic cigarette, it started to feel fairly natural, and after two days it was a part of my life as much as any conventional cigarette without any real effort.

I continued to use the electronic cigarette for at least a month while my mind worked in the background to solve the problem of where to go from here.

It was then that I discovered the next course of action I would take to beat the habit for for good.

I bought some nicotine gum from a local pharmacist, plus here's the key, some regular gum as well. As I've mentioned before, most nicotine replacement gum for me, tastes really bad, so the regular gum was to make it palatable and not to stick in my throat.

Once I had the gum, I found the courage to switch to a half dose refill of the electronic cigarette, i.e. half the amount of nicotine, and then supplemented the missing nicotine with a piece of nicotine gum and a supporting piece of regular gum. So I'd smoke a bit of the electronic cigarette and then chew a piece of both types of gum to get the extra nicotine.

My experience with the gum was far better than any other before it. The regular gum made the intake of nicotine so much easier. The satisfaction from the gum was clear and I'd often experience a buzz after chewing it, similar to the head rush of smoking a cigarette and sometimes also a pleasant buzzing sensation in my mouth and tongue.

The process was working. And I was excited about it. I did that for some time but was eager to move on and experience more success in reducing my nicotine intake.

After a short time, I started to cut the pieces of nicotine gum in half to reduce the dose every alternate smoking session. Sometimes, I'd have to chew two halves if I still felt irritable, but the halving formula was always the same. Eventually I got used to the new half dose in my regular daily routine and then started making plans to switch to a nicotine free smoking mixture for the electronic cigarette.

This was a daunting move and required a bit of courage, but as always, I didn't do it until I was ready. When I did, there was a significant difference, but to keep the nicotine intake into the body steady, I again chewed more nicotine gum, much more than I needed so I didn't experience any withdrawal and also to reward me psychologically.

By now, the process had started to become a lot of fun. I'd buy different flavoured chewing gums of brands I'd never tried before and mix them with the nicotine gum. I started to enjoy certain flavours more than others and also the sensation that some of the different flavours had, particularly the minty ones. Unknowingly, I had also started to link my oral fixation and addiction to a new platform, the chewing gum instead of the cigarette.

I was now in a place where I was smoking a harmless vapour and only getting nicotine from the chewing gum. I knew I was on the verge of victory. It was just these final steps and I would have beaten this for good.

What followed would be considered by some as utter madness. I cut the nicotine gum in quarters. I found myself smoking the nicotine free electronic cigarette and chewing some gum with a quarter piece of nicotine for a few weeks. The dose was enough to keep me from getting irritable.

One day, I was at an airport and I ran out of the mixture that fuelled my electronic cigarette. I fell back on my quarter piece nicotine gum mixture and sometimes ate two of those to reward myself for the psychological victory of only using the gum. After my trip, I never bought a refill for the e-cigarette and I found myself being able to chew only the gum and being comfortable doing that. That became my new routine, and it was also something I could do anytime, meaning I didn't have to be outside to chew gum.

I started alternating between regular gum and the quarter nicotine gum mix as and when I was ready until I could manage only three doses a day. Morning, noon, and night. Those I gradually reduced to two and then to one a day, until I attempted a nicotine free day.

I remember waking up after having one day of success under my belt. It was clear that the next goal was to make seven days. Then I knew I was in the clear. Seven days passed. And then eight, nine, and ten. And there were no withdrawal symptoms. Every day that passed made me feel happier and stronger, I had accomplished my goal. In my mind I had done the impossible. The affect this had on my psyche, was phenomenal.

Psychologically, I had associated chewing gum as a replacement for smoking, with the support of the nicotine gum. With the dosage gradually reduced to zero, my mind accepted the routine as an acceptable alternative to smoking.

I chewed a lot of gum over the next few months. And it worked and continued to work.

Four years later, I had no desire to smoke, except I had a strange side effect from my process of quitting. I'd still see chewing gum as a guilty pleasure and find myself enjoying it as much as any smoker would enjoy a good cigarette.

So. About that oral fixation.. I continued to chew gum for some time afterwards. Religiously. One day, I just got tired of it and stopped. If I got irritable, I'd fall back on the habit, but in general I found it just wasn't necessary anymore.

CHAPTER 4

Having gone through this journey, at times it seems surreal. I was a non-smoker.

It just happened, and looking back, the events I described seemed to have passed by in the blink of an eye. Some interesting things started to take place in my life, some that could be considered positive and other which were quite challenging.

One of the challenging aspects of this process was my attitude towards people that still smoked. If I walked past an area at work that was frequented by smokers, I would pass by groups of people I usually smoked with and found my way of interacting with them challenging. I didn't want to be rude or change my attitude towards them, so I'd stop and say hi and then be exposed to the fumes of cigarette smoke which were at this point now repulsive to me.

This ended very quickly, as I was not going to compromise my integrity or what I had worked for, so I developed some new strategies for dealing with these situations. I started to walk with far more purpose in my steps. On my way to work, I was a man on a mission and instead of stopping for a conversation, I walked past quickly, clear that I had some purpose I was attending to, greeted the people cheerfully and went into the building. After time, this became a natural state of behaviour and truth be told, no-one cared or noticed. Looking back, I find it silly, but this was a real challenge for me at the time.

Another was accepting a lunch invitation with a colleague of mine. After a good meal at a street café, they lit an after-meal cigarette and I was amazed at how little consideration they had for my predicament.

In hindsight I can't imagine they would have known or had empathy for what I was going through. I remember times where I was smoking, and someone complained about my cigarette smoke laughing at them behind their backs. It became absolutely amazing to me how inconsiderate smokers could be about a common space we share; in the air we breathe. The only thing I could do was to manage my interactions more to avoid these situations until I was no longer bothered by them.

At the time, I didn't think that would happen to be honest. The plan was to avoid all smokers forever, so I didn't have to experience that again. As time passed and my own resolve became greater backed by every month that passed without smoking, I started to enjoy seeing if I could withstand temptation and would test myself around people smoking, just to see what I would do and how I would feel. Nowadays I can even go to a dingy pool bar without the smoke bugging me and I still have no desire to smoke.

Unfortunately, some relationships I had did change during this period. Some ended. The transition phase of moving into different habits can be challenging for all involved. I can only speak for myself and say that it does pass. More personal relationships, especially romantic ones can be challenging if you share space. Perhaps the only thing you can do is hope that these people are inspired by your change.

A third challenge I experienced was that after a good few months after completely quitting, I experienced what I can only describe as a remarkable averageness of everything. I didn't have the highs that nicotine gave me every hour or so, so at times, the world seemed to be for me a chain of experiences that were all equal in nature. As time passed, I started to find new joys in aspects of my life which were far subtler than I could perceive before, and started to really learn things about who I really am, what I like and what I want to do with my life.

Another one of the positive changes I experienced were increased purpose. At first it seemed like there was just too much time in the day and I had too much time on my hands. I needed to take regular breaks at work, drinking lots of cups of tea or coffee to pass time or just having to move to a new area of the building I was in for a change of scenery.

This passed fairly quickly and I found myself having so many great ideas in the months to follow, that eventually, there wasn't enough time in the day. I started lots of small projects I wanted to see evolve and would work on them in small amounts furthering each one, but never working on one long enough to lose my enthusiasm. Again, I was experimenting, seeing where I would go and what I would do from here. Some ideas stayed with me in the long time, some didn't.

A second positive change was the change in my skin. Having smoked a pack a day for almost sixteen years, my skin was an olive ash colour. I never really noticed until one day my younger sister showed me a photograph of myself, one taken a few years back and I was pretty shocked at the difference. It still pains me to look at those photos today. I genuinely feel sorry for myself back then.

Another plus was the cleanliness of not having to smoke. My house was cleaner; my curtains didn't smell like tobacco; I had no more need for ashtrays. I was cleaner too. My fingers didn't smell like tobacco. My lungs seemed to clear themselves out and I got rid of a smoker's cough and constant clearing of my throat which I imagine was my lungs constantly clearing out impurities from smoking.

What amazed me is that most smokers don't seem to realise they have this at all. They say it's not a smoker's cough, it's just a cough. That constant clearing of the lungs and throat seems to be strangely invisible.

My sense of taste was moderately affected. After a year of not smoking, I didn't enjoy certain foods anymore. It was nothing earth shattering, but I stopped liking a certain wheaty cereal and mayonnaise. As time moved on, this returned to normal, but overall, I can't honestly say my sense of taste hasn't changed that much.

Another positive of this process was physical fitness. To pass time, I started to enjoy new activities and took up some light running, mixed martial arts training and whatever else I felt like at the time. At first, I did it because I would have probably gone mad with the surge of new energy I was experiencing, but later, this evened out and it felt more natural and relaxed.

There was one last experience for me that personally made me feel I had crossed over for good. This was a uniquely personal experience, and I can't imagine that anyone else would experience exactly the same thing, but one night, I was sleeping and dreaming that I was smoking a cigarette, but I had the lungs of a new-born child. The experience was so revolting and so intense that I woke up. The only way I can describe this feeling is to imagine that you forced a new-born baby to inhale a lungful of the hardest unfiltered cigarette you could possibly find and then imagine its reaction. This experience was for me extremely profound and vivid and I knew deep down that this was the marker for me and I would never go back.

CHAPTER 5

In the past few chapters, I've done the best I can to take you on the journey with me so you could experience it without worrying too much about the method. Now that we've done that, we can begin to explore what actually happened a little closer.

Many people associate quitting smoking with suffering. Smokers often feel a pain in their lungs when they go too long without a cigarette and then anxiety, irritability and often far worse symptoms the longer they go without their nicotine fix.

In the process that unfolded for me, I never once experienced something that was too far out of my comfort zone and instead of a sudden drop, sailed in home for a smooth and easy landing, gradually and in my own time. My sense of pride an accomplishment in achieving this has been so gratifying for me and empowering too.

So, let's have a look at what you can do to start setting this in motion. As you can tell, the method is not cast in stone but has some guidelines. These guidelines are:

To not overexert yourself straining to take bigger steps than you are ready for.

To have the freedom to smoke whenever you want to until you say it is over.

To gradually reduce your nicotine intake slowly and gradually over a long-term period. This can be for as long as you need. For me it was between four to six months.

To increase your nicotine intake again if you experience any uncomfortable withdrawal symptoms.

To supplement your body with an increase of oxygen by doing some light cycling or gym. Take care not to overexert, so you can keep coming back. Smaller work sessions frequently are better than one power session to overcompensate for your lack of fitness and you never come back. 20mins of light cycling, jogging a day for example. Go for a walk instead if you find this hard. Get your body moving.

For me, I found that these were the essentials steps:

The purchasing of an electronic cigarette brand that has full strength, half strength and zero nicotine options.

The gradual decrease of nicotine absorbed by regular cigarettes, by alternating smoking habits between two brands of cigarettes with different strengths equally divided into two boxes.

The repetition of this first step until your nicotine intake becomes at least a quarter of your original intake. If you are already smoking a really light brand, you might consider the electronic cigarette as an immediate option and alternate between that and your regular brand.

Switching over to the e-cigarette when you are ready.

The supplementing of nicotine intake via the use of a nicotine replacement gum, masked with other regular flavoured gum. This for me was the winning formula that made nicotine replacement gum palatable.

It may seem simple if you look at these steps from a distance, and it is, however, just be aware that living them is very different. You may find that you invent your own adaptations along the way or deviate from the method above. The important thing is that it feels right for you, so don't be afraid to experiment.

As above, you may already smoke a light brand of cigarette. You could try alternating between that and an e-ciggarette. As an incentive there, eliminating those extra harmful chemicals can be a motivating factor to try and start.

Always key here, is to allow yourself to go back. Until you are ready to go forward. At your own pace, involve no-one else in that decision making.

So, having understood the method in a little more detail, here's what you can do about it.

No-one is going to force you to quit or have a ceremonial last cigarette or make any promises to anyone. You might not even find any measure of success for some time. But so what. What you can do, is to the next time you buy a box of cigarettes, but two instead. One full strength, and one half your usual strength. When you get home, divide these evenly in two packs and go about your day.

Next time you walk past a tobacco store or retailer that has them, buy an electronic cigarette too.

From here, make the decision to casually see what happens and enjoy the process.

Conclusion

After around eight years of quitting smoking, I'd like to share with you what has happened in my life.

I don't want to paint a picture of paradise filled with rainbows and unicorns for the sake of this book, but I can say my life is pretty awesome. And I am so much happier.

With all the extra time and energy I've had, I started drawing again. As a creative, this was something I never found time for, but I started to perfect my drawing and digital painting skills.

Over the next few years, that passion developed into a much bigger story and the creation of a formal concept art education program which teaches skills geared towards creating art for film games and animation. This has been one of the most fulfilling accomplishments of my life so far, and at the time of making my last edits, not a week or two ago, I hosted a graduation ceremony for my students issuing the first accredited concept art qualifications in Africa.

Moving forward now, I can only look forward to creating new things and finding new ways to offer value to others. I hope my next contribution will be in the arts developing a product or campaign that is loved worldwide and appreciated for its quality.

I don't want to over glamourise how important quitting smoking was in setting these events in motion but will rather say it was definitely key in my personal journey to becoming more self-actualised, and for me that means becoming a person that is far more on track with their dreams and why they are really here on the planet to do.

If this book moves you towards the same path in some way, then I have offered value to the world in ways I can't even begin to imagine and that is for me truly exciting.